Monique

Happy 42nd

Love Dale + Carol

A GOOD

Swing

IS HARD
TO FIND

———

A GOOD

Swing

IS HARD

TO FIND

HOW WOMEN CAN
PLAY THE POWER GAME

HELEN ALFREDSSON
WITH AMY ELLIS NUTT

DOUBLEDAY

NEW YORK   LONDON   TORONTO   SYDNEY   AUCKLAND

PUBLISHED BY DOUBLEDAY
a division of Bantam Doubleday Dell Publishing Group,
Inc.
1540 Broadway, New York, New York 10036

DOUBLEDAY and the portrayal of an anchor with a dolphin
are trademarks of Doubleday, a division of
Bantam Doubleday Dell Publishing Group, Inc.

Book design by Donna Sinisgalli

Library of Congress Cataloging-in-Publication Data
Alfredsson, Helen.
A good swing is hard to find : how women can play the power game /
by Helen Alfredsson with Amy Ellis Nutt. — 1st ed.
p.   cm.
1. Golf for women.   2. Swing (Golf)   I. Nutt, Amy Ellis.
II. Title.
GV966.A44   1998
796.352′3′082—dc21   97-52697
CIP

ISBN 0-385-48821-1

May 1998

First Edition

10 9 8 7 6 5 4 3 2 1

To Leo, for always being there.

Acknowledgments

My thanks go way back, to Alan Anderton, my first golf teacher in Göteborg; to Thure Holmström, coach of the Swedish National Team; and to Barbro Montgomery, captain of the National Team. Also, to Amy for all the good times. To Scott Waxman of the Scott Waxman Agency, and Rob Robertson, who started this book on its way, and to Denell Downum of Doubleday, who saw it to the finish line. Finally, to my family, my love and thanks for standing by me through good times and bad.

Contents

Introduction   1

1   Kick Out the Jams: The Value of Having a Light
    Heart   7

2   All Shook Up: How to Deal with Fear   14

3   You Can't Always Get What You Want: Dealing
    with Anger   21

4   Walk on the Wild Side: And Get to Know Yourself   26

5   Be the Ball: The Concentration Game   31

6   Whatever Gets You Through the Night: The Value
    of a Distraction   34

7   No Surrender: The Power of Positive Thinking   37

8   It Don't Come Easy: The Value of Reality Testing   42

9   Get Up, Stand Up: Learning from Your Mistakes   45

10 Takin' Care of Business: Making the Shot When You
Need It Most   49

11 Swing Time: Legs Are a Girl's Best Friend   54

12 Hard Habit to Break: Know Your Right Side, But
Don't Overdo It   60

13 Get Back: The Power in Staying Behind the Ball   64

14 Get a Grip: Knuckle Up, Not Under   .   70

15 The Rhythm Method: Slower Is Better   74

16 How to Stay on the Straight and Narrow: And Avoid
Going over the Top   79

17 The One True Thing: All About Aim   83

18 Feel, Trust, Deliver: The Pre-Shot Routine   87

19 The Option Plan: How to Think Your Way Around
the Course   91

20 Did You Ever Have to Make Up Your Mind?:
Playing the Percentages   96

21 Of Shafts and Sweet Spots: Choosing the Right
Equipment   99

22 Every Breath You Take: Exercising Your Way to
Better Golf   104

23 A Good Man Is Hard to Find: Golf and the
Opposite Sex   109

24 It's Still Rock and Roll to Me: Final Thought   114

A GOOD

Swing

IS HARD

TO FIND

———

Introduction

I want to tell you, right off, that this is *not* another boring golf book. It is not about the fifty-six reasons to eschew the interlocking grip. Nor is it about the one true path toward a more perfect address. What this book *is* about I can say in three words: *full throttle golf.*

So what the hell is full throttle golf, you ask? It's about playing with power and confidence, but also humor and fun. It's about being who you are out on the golf course, not who some staid golf manual says you should be. It's about driving for show *and* driving for dough, if you and your partners are so inclined. Finally, it's about being competitive, about unleashing the tiger that is within you.

When I think of tigers in the wild, I think about how strong they are and how self-sufficient. Nobody else is going to take care of them, so they have to go after everything they need or want themselves. I believe that this is also the best way to play golf, whether you're a man or a woman. No one else can make the shot for you and you certainly can't win if you don't first believe that you can. When you know what you want, you have to trust yourself that you have what it takes to get to the finish line.

My fiancé, Leo Cuellar, first used the phrase "unleash the tiger" the week after the 1994 U.S. Open at Indianwood Golf and Country Club in Lake Orion, Michigan. That year I became the first woman ever to shoot a 63 in an Open and the first man or woman to reach 13 under par—but I eventually lost the championship to Patty Sheehan. It was pretty crushing at the time—winning a U.S. Open is probably the greatest accomplishment any golfer can have and I hope someday to achieve it—but I vowed not to let the loss deter me.

The week after losing the Open, I found myself once again in a position to win at the Ping Welch's championship outside of Boston. After making the turn on the last day of the tournament, I realized I was in a fight to the finish with two of the great players on the LPGA Tour, Juli Inkster and Hall of Famer Pat Bradley. When I birdied the tenth hole to go into a three-way tie, I knew right then that it was make or break time. I didn't want to do what I did at the Open and Leo must have read my mind. He came up to me and said, "Okay honey, come on, it's time to unleash the tiger."

I birdied four out of the next seven holes for a back nine 31 and a final round score of 66, enough to win the tournament by four strokes. I had unleashed the tiger; I had played the game the way I knew I could. I had no fear. I was aggressive and I went for the stick. I hung tough. And it worked.

I've always tried to live my life without regret, to go for what I wanted and not to leave anything in the tank. I've had great opportunities to do this in areas outside of golf, as well. Last year I flew with the elite Navy group the Blue Angels. We hit 700 mph—just under the sound barrier—and did a near vertical ascent with seven G-forces squashing me back into my seat. We also did aerial loops, dives and a simulated bombing run. It was one of the biggest thrills of my life. And I didn't even throw up!

A couple of years ago I also had a chance to drag-race at Daytona Raceway in Daytona Beach, Florida. I took a class (and earned my racing license) along with five PGA Tour players, including Davis Love III and Bruce Lietzke. And then I went out and beat all of them on the drag strip. Take my word for it, to go from zero to 164 miles an hour in less than six seconds is absolutely *otroligt*! (that's Swedish for "unbelievable!"). So, yes, I love speed, and though many of my friends are afraid to get in a car with me, I have never had an accident. For that matter, I have never even had a speeding ticket—although back in my hometown I do know most of the policemen and policewomen by name.

It is definitely true that because I am a professional athlete, I get chances to do things most people don't, but everybody has the chance to live life to the fullest, which is what it's all about as far as I'm concerned. This is how I play golf, too, and how I think more people, both men and women, should play the game: without excuses, with fun, with power and, above all, always at full throttle.

I wanted to convey all these things in a new kind of book about golf. And I especially wanted to address myself to women golfers. In the past, too many books for the female golfer dwelt mainly on technique, and rarely on distance or power. But if you've been following the LPGA Tour at all for the past few years, you should know by now that women can, and do, play with power. With better physical training and better equipment, women golfers—and not just the pros—are learning to use their drivers, their woods and their long irons, and are not apologizing for it. So the tips that I give in this book are mainly for those who want to put a little more muscle into their swing and get a lot more out of their game.

This book, however, is not just about the new power game, but about how to enjoy being competitive at the same time. And while you're being competitive, how to also have fun.

Because I'm what is called a "feel" player, I want to teach you how to do for yourself some of the things golfers often take for granted or simply overlook. Like visualizing your target, having a pre-shot routine, thinking your way around a golf course, judging what club to take and also how to create the shot you need, and perhaps most important, taking care of your game not only physically and technically, but mentally as well.

Maybe the most important bit of advice in this book is about how to find your own emotional comfort zone out on the golf course: recognizing what works best for you in how you approach and play the game. I've never believed in cookie-cutter golf. For me, golf isn't about always being serious and grinding out each of my rounds. It isn't about being a robot out on the golf course or about always having to keep everything under wraps emotionally. I'm not like that in life and I can't be like that in golf.

I really believe that sometimes you can be too much in control and therefore not open to being creative or to having fun. Striving always to wear the same game face is one of those traditional beliefs in sports that I question. That's not me and never has been. I've had to accept who I am out on the golf course—emotional, fiery and yes, sometimes just a bit crazy. But I've found out for me that it's better to be expressive than to try and hold everything in.

Anyone who plays the game, no matter at what level, needs to find out who they are and what they're like out on the golf course and then honor that. Instead of feeling forced to always act and react a certain way, we each need to find out what works best for us as individuals. It used to be that women acting aggressive or competitive in sports—especially in golf—was a no-no. Not anymore.

So my first recommendation is: throw away those pink golf bags, ladies, and definitely those golf skirts. (I tried wearing one once and let me tell you, I never knew that bending down to pick up a golf ball could be so complicated and so risqué!). No more thinking you always have to lay up. No more always holding back. Be a little bit daring for a change. Maybe even try the blue tees. Empty the tank. Put the pedal to the metal. Be yourself. And let's rock and roll.

1

Kick Out the Jams

THE VALUE OF HAVING A LIGHT HEART

I hate to admit this, but golfers are a pretty boring lot. I don't know if this is because the sport is so all-consuming, or if it's because we've all been browbeaten with the old bromide that the less emotional you are, the more successful you'll be on a golf course. Frankly I think that's about as smart as a five-wood out of waist-high fescue. Golf shouldn't be like church—silent, solemn and stiff-collared. There are already way too many golfers who act like tax accountants, an overabundance of men in plaid pants and more than a few women who color-coordinate their clothes with their head covers.

Instructional books, too, have taken on a whole other kind of technical seriousness, so that any reader who actually gets through one should automatically receive college credits. What a lot of linkslanders have forgotten is that while golf may have a bit of Bach in its precision and complexity, it also has a whole lot of rock and roll in the creativity and spontaneity that you must have to play it well.

Now don't get me wrong. I think golf is a very serious sport and I take great pride in the fact that it is how I make my living. But a serious sport doesn't have to be—shouldn't be—played so seriously all the time. I am living proof that if you have a tendency to talk to yourself, tell off-color jokes to unsuspecting strangers and prefer the music of Bush to Bach, you may still have a very good chance of becoming an excellent golfer. In fact, the first thing I do whenever I get to a new tournament is find the best rock station on the car radio. After being on the LPGA Tour for six years, I can tell you that I know exactly which ones to tune in to when I arrive at each site.

This is just the way I am. All my life I have been called names, like "crazy" (by my college golf coach), "wacky" (by friends on tour) and the "Swede with the need for speed" (by the press). Most of it is true. When I was at U.S. International University in San Diego, I studied hard, but I also partied hard, and I was kicked off the golf team three times. I just wanted to be my own person. When my coach gave me a personality test, he was a bit horrified by the results, which he said showed I was "uncoachable." To me, it meant that I was opinionated, that I spoke my mind and that if I knew something was right for me, but not necessarily for another player, well, I had to follow my own rules.

I also filled out a personality profile for the Swedish Golf

Federation before I became a professional. There were only two ways of scoring the answers. The responses to the questions were either given an "S"—which meant the answer indicated a supposedly Swedish quality, like "is quiet," "follows orders" and "is mild-mannered"—or a "P"—which meant any non-Swedish qualities. As you no doubt have already guessed, I had zero "S" marks, and all "P's." My Swedish coach was so nonplussed she made me take the test a second time!

Okay, so I admit it, I'm a high-octane person. My family calls me the energizer bunny, because I just keep going and going and going. In grade school I couldn't stop talking, so my teachers were always making up special rules for me, like I had to sit directly in front of the blackboard, and if I felt like laughing, I had to go outside for a five-minute break. My problem was, I was bored. Which is one reason why I love golf so much—it's endlessly interesting and endlessly challenging.

Given who I am, I guess it stands to reason that when I want to relax, it's usually at high speed. Yes, I own a Harley, and I have my drag racing license, and I hope to earn a pilot's license soon, too. I know plenty of pros who like to fish, others who collect antiques or like to garden or watch sports on TV. I like to get my heart racing. Believe it or not, I feel calmest when I'm pushing the envelope.

The point I'm trying to make here—and there is a point—is that sometimes it's actually good for your golf

GOLF, to me, is a full-throttle sport. And the only way to approach it is to be yourself and follow your own rules for what works best for *you* out on the course.

game to push the envelope, to be spontaneous, to be aggressive and to have fun at the same time. I remember reading once how if people regard you as crazy or eccentric, then they're less likely to expect you to act in a certain way. This can work to your advantage: if others give you more leeway with your behavior, then you will give yourself more leeway, too.

So, my first bit of advice to you, since you bought this book and not some other one, is to loosen up. Be bold. Experiment. And above all, relax and have fun. I read something once about the former U.S. skier Debbie Armstrong, who won an Olympic gold medal in the giant slalom in 1984. When she was in the starting gate, she would psych herself up by chanting: "Have fun! Have fun! Have fun!" That was her way of trying to stay loose before a big race, but it also illustrates what I think is the only attitude you should have when playing any sport. If it ain't fun, why bother?

I try and stay so focused week in and week out because I don't want anything to interfere with my concentration on my game. But then all of a sudden this little devil comes crawling out, saying, "It's time to do something. You've been good too long." I know then that I have to loosen up a bit, sit back and try to enjoy not only the golf, but my life, just a bit more.

I learned an important lesson about having the right attitude when I was still a teenager in Sweden. I was expecting to go to the World Amateur Championships, but the Swedish Golf Federation selected another player. I was crushed. Instead, I was selected to play in the less prestigious junior internationals in Belgium. At first, I didn't want to go. I sulked and decided I didn't want to play golf ever again. I did go, of course, and went to bed early before the first round. But the next day I played awful, and shot something like 80. So that night I decided what the hell and I stayed out until 3 A.M. partying. I did the same thing for the next two nights as well. And do you know what happened? That's right, I won the tournament!

This may be a particular talent of the women in my country, because I have a friend who once did much the same thing. We were playing in the Scandinavian Match Play tournament in Norway and this friend of mine was in the final twosome going into the final day. Her opponent, also from Sweden, went to bed early like a good girl, but my wild friend stayed out all night. In fact, she showed up at the course the next day in the same clothes she'd had on the day before! And yep, you guessed it, she won, too.

I have tremendous respect for the game of golf and its history and I do take my role as a professional player very seriously. After all, golf is my career. But one thing I've learned since I picked up the game at the age of eleven is that you can be serious about the game without being overly serious about playing it. There are too many uptight people in the world and certainly too many uptight golfers. I think it's more important for your game that you express yourself out on the golf course, that you joke, or talk with other players, that you stay loose. Who knows, even when you might not be hitting the ball well, you may still find yourself having fun. And when you're having fun, you're usually playing better golf.

2

All Shook Up

How to Deal with Fear

Franklin Roosevelt wasn't the only one in the family who spoke about fear when he said those now oft repeated words, "The only thing we have to fear is fear itself." His wife Eleanor also spoke on the subject, though not quite as tersely. "You gain strength, courage and confidence," she wrote toward the end of her life, "by every experience in which you really stop to look fear in the face."

Every golfer, at one time or another in his or her life, has walked up to a shot and just wanted to run away and hide. I know I have. In fact, there have been times when I thought I might even throw up, what with all the anxiety. It doesn't matter if you're standing over a slippery six-foot putt to win a major or stepping up to the first tee with a group of guys eyeing your every move. Panic is an equal opportunity emotion. I don't know a single golfer, pro or amateur, who hasn't had to deal with fear on the golf course.

We've all had to deal with those funky thoughts in our head, those voices that speak the unspeakable: "You're going to miss this putt" or "You know you can't get this to the hole" or worse, "You don't even know how to swing that club." And the more you try to brush the voices aside, the louder they scream at you.

The key to dealing with all fears is to recognize them for what they are. I don't actually mean for you to scream out "I'm going to miss this putt!" I simply mean that you have to acknowledge the voices in order to handle them. Don't ignore them and don't try to disown your panic. Instead, own up to the fear, tell yourself, "Yeah, I'm scared, I'm worried I might not make this next shot, but I don't care."

Golf is one of those rare sports where you have to learn to care just enough but not too much. Care too much and the fear and the panic and the desire to hit the perfect shot will overwhelm you. If that's not a recipe for failure, I don't know what is.

My mother, Kathie, is a great example—and a funny one—of what fear and anxiety on a golf course can do to you. My mother was for many years a champion bowler back home in Göteborg, Sweden. I grew up going to her tournaments, and in turn, she would come out to watch me play junior golf.

About fifteen years ago, my mother played in her first golf tournament. The tournament took place at our home course, Gullbringa Country Club, and my mother, who is a smoker (I've tried to get her to quit many times), was extremely nervous as she waited to tee off. In fact, she was smoking up a storm and when her name was called to play away, she bent down to tee up her ball and suddenly realized her tee was in her mouth and she was trying to stick her cigarette into the ground!

As if that wasn't bad enough, when my mother got to the first green she panicked again, because she now realized she had nothing with which to mark her ball. Just then, "eureka!," she found a marker already on the green. Naturally, she picked it up and used it. There was only one problem: the marker belonged to her playing partner.

In golf, just as in life, we try to ignore the bad things that are happening to us, our fear, the proverbial pink elephant in the living room that everyone pretends isn't really there. If we're lucky, we just end up doing silly things, as my mother did, but difficult emotions can be tenacious unless we face up to them. Fear and anxiety usually don't go away on their own, or at least not before they leave a lot of damage in their wake. And usually they get a whole lot worse until we finally acknowledge them.

The fear that we experience in golf is always going to be there, even if it's just the fear of embarrassment. But if we can see fear for what it is, accept it and acknowledge it, then we can move on. When that voice in my head says I'm not going to make that putt, there's nothing else to do but accept the possibility that I might not—and then try to make it anyway. If I tell myself I care just enough and not too much it takes away a lot of the pressure.

One of the big problems with finding yourself in the throes of fear and anxiety is that you lose perspective. All of a sudden, your past failures, or imagined failures, loom large in your mind. You begin to think you've never done anything but fail and your brain seems to be telling you that the same fate awaits you now at every turn, with every big putt, every pressure drive.

One way to prevent the fear from escalating is to remember positive past experiences and successes. The time you made a big putt or placed a perfect drive on the last hole of a big round. Even when you find yourself in a new situation, having to make a shot you've never had to make before, you can draw on some positive aspect from a similar experience. Picture a previous shot that was successful, a putt that dropped in from thirty feet, a chip that left you six inches from the hole. Doing this will create a groundswell of confidence that will help relieve the fear and stem the rising anxiety.

When you are faced with a high-pressure shot, sometimes just asking yourself, "What's the worst that could happen?" is a big help. Usually the answer is "Well, I'll miss the putt or hook my drive out of bounds, or I'll whiff the ball." In the greater context of things, these are pretty minor events. They never seem minor when you're in the middle of them, but if you can step out of the situation for just a moment, you can gain just the bit of distance you may need to relax yourself.

When football coaches or baseball managers call a time-out it's usually to give their players a break, a chance to regroup, calm down and assess the state of the game. You can do the same thing for yourself when you are in the clutch of a tough putt. When you stop to ask the question "What's the worst that could happen?" you're assessing your own situation, calming down, regrouping and figuring out what to do. Mental time-outs are crucial to preserving not only your game but, frankly, your sanity.

One thing I always try to do when I'm feeling overwhelmed by anxiety on the course is to go through a little routine of tensing my hands for a couple of seconds, and then shaking them out to relax them. You can create a similar ritual with any simple, repetitive movement that helps you to calm down.

It's easy to say, "Just relax," but many people don't know a thing about how to actually get themselves to relax. Physiologically, when we're anxious we are not breathing in enough oxygen, which is why our extremities (hands and feet) start to go numb.

So the main thing to do when you're feeling tense and you need to relax is to think about breathing more slowly.

You first want to be sure not to just use the upper part of your chest, but to breathe from your stomach. Let your stomach expand as you breathe in deeply, holding your breath for a count of three, and then exhaling slowly and evenly, watching your stomach empty. You'll not only find your brain getting more oxygen, but the rest of your body will feel more relaxed as well.

Before you go out and play, while you're still sitting in your car, or the ladies' locker room, or the grill, you might want to try this relaxation exercise. After all, a dash of Zen never hurt anyone's game.

Each time you breathe, tense a group of muscles and count to three. Then, while you breathe out, whisper the word "calm" and let those muscles go limp. Start with your feet, then your calves, your thighs, your buttocks. Slowly move up to your stomach, chest and shoulders. Do the same with your arms and hands and then move up to your neck, and even your face muscles. Let your head drop down and roll it around a full 360 degrees.

After you've relaxed your entire body, from toe to head, do one final drill. Count down from ten to one. With each deep breath, count off a number; as you exhale, whisper the word "calmer." Repeat this until you get down to the number one. Then take a final couple of minutes and imagine yourself in a very relaxing place: you're lying on a tropical beach; sitting by a babbling brook; in the sweetest-smelling garden; or dozing in a rocking chair on a porch in the summer twilight. You should now be completely relaxed—maybe you've even fallen asleep for a few seconds, which is okay. The point is, you're now ready to take on the world, including those three men you've just been paired with!

3

You Can't Always Get What You Want

DEALING WITH ANGER

Chances are, if you're not throwing up before a shot, you're throwing a club after one. Next to fear, anger is probably *the* most difficult emotion to deal with on the golf course. Believe me, I should know. The golf commentators use words for me like "fiery," "emotional," "expressive" when what they really want to say is "Man, she's angrier than a bulldog in a box of bees." And it's true, anger is the one emotion with which I still have an unsteady relationship.

Although I believe it's important for me to express myself and not to hold back, I've had to learn some lessons about when not to become angry while on the golf course. Once, when I was fourteen or fifteen years old, my dad walked off the course when he was caddying for me in a local tournament. I'd been angry and sarcastic with myself on about fourteen of the fifteen holes I'd played. I was saying things like "Oh, that's perfect, it's in the water" or "Great, you cannot putt to save your life." Finally he threw down the bag and told me he'd had enough, I should carry my own clubs or "just go to hell." He walked off and I had to carry my clubs for the remaining three holes.

My father had every right to do what he did. I behaved terribly and was disrespectful toward him when he was there to be supportive. And when he left me out there on the sixteenth tee, he told me basically that if that was how I was going to act, he didn't want to be a part of it.

Another time, at my first junior national championship in Sweden, when I was about nine years old, I was playing well and was close to the lead after the first nine holes. But I finished the first round of thirty-six holes taking a 10 on the eighteenth. I cried and told my father I didn't want to play golf anymore—*ever*—and my dad said, well, you have to, you don't have a choice in the matter. He said I had an afternoon tee time and that my attitude was ridiculous. "This is what happens when you play golf," I remember him saying. "It might be the first time, but it certainly won't be the last." He expected me to step up to the plate, go out and face whatever was out there for me. He was right again. And that's what I continue to try to do today even when my golf is not going very well. I know that I have to suck it up and play on. I haven't walked off a course yet (though I sometimes still want to).

Facing up to anger and disappointment still isn't easy for me. There are any number of players who don't get as easily ruffled out there as I do, but my style has never been particularly low key. I think that's why a lot of amateur golfers—both male and female—seem to identify with me. They see that I get angry with stupid shots, too. But I try not to let the anger control me. Just as with fear, you can't bury your anger and you can't ignore it.

I like to think that I keep control of my anger. I know I can't keep it all in, but I also know I can't always let it all hang out. You can't get angry with *everything* on the golf course, otherwise you'll simply self-destruct.

In my first year on tour in 1992 I was at a tournament in San Diego and everything seemed to be going wrong. First of all, I was dealing with PMS while trying to play golf—never a good combination. Second, I couldn't make heads or tails out of the yardage book. My irritation threshold was very low—if anybody so much as sneezed, it bothered me. And here I was walking down the fairway with no idea of the distances because I couldn't find the yardage markers. I remember being in a long bunker and after I hit out I told Leo, who was caddying for me, to get the rake, which was all the way at the back of the bunker, and fix the sand. I wasn't sure he'd heard me—or maybe he was ignoring me—so I said again, this time with a bit more irritation in my voice, "Why don't you get the friggin' rake." With that, Leo turned to me and said in the most evenhanded way, "So what were you doing in there in the first place?" To which, of course, I had absolutely no reply. Touché.

Anger, we all know, is one of those emotions that releases adrenaline into the bloodstream—just as when you are afraid or anxious. Adrenaline is basically poison for a golfer. Too much adrenaline and your heart will begin to pump so much that you aren't able to control anything on the course anymore. You start doing everything faster, swinging harder and tensing up muscles that are supposed to stay supple and relaxed.

But if you can get angry and then get over it fairly quickly you will be okay. I'm a passionate person. I live life and I live golf in the same way. I feel that if I talk to the ball, or to myself, it might help. When I hit a bad shot because of a stupid swing, I don't try to suppress my anger. I let my temper flare and I yell at myself. Or I slam my club down on my foot—I've bruised a few toes in my time. But then I always move on. I leave the anger behind me; I don't carry it over to the next hole. I'm sure it's largely because I do express my anger, rather than bottling it up inside, that I'm able to let it go.

In golf you are always supposed to be in control. I get letters sometimes from people who say I shouldn't show so much emotion, but I've won more than a dozen tournaments worldwide and this is the way I've always been. Unfortunately, golf is not a sport where you can wear your anger on your sleeve, as in football or basketball, where anger can actually improve your play. You can't go running down the fairway shouting at your ball in a golf tournament.

But the fact is, every golfer gets mad at their game at one time or another. Yelling at my ball or swearing (in Swedish, so I don't get fined) is a definite release, like letting the steam out from under a boiling pot so the hot water doesn't spill over. Once, a British writer said of my penchant for verbal outbursts, "They can be louder and more richly worded than many of Lenny Bruce's best performances." I have news for that guy: I also feel a whole lot better afterward.

I've had to learn over the years not to get upset every single time I do something wrong. I realized it was just wasted energy when I became angry with the thousands of small frustrations that occur on a golf course. But expressing anger will clear out the cobwebs and you can use all that raw emotion to light a fire under yourself. Learn to channel your anger by refocusing on your next shot. The key to breaking the hold of anger is to know what part of it is helpful, and what part is not. I'm still learning the differences every day. One thing I know for sure is that you can't stay angry with yourself. And you can't pity yourself, either. Bill Walsh, who used to coach my favorite football team, the '49ers, once said that if you give up you never have a chance.

4

Walk on the Wild Side

AND GET TO KNOW YOURSELF

Do you remember the old TV series *Lost in Space,* with the robot that always seemed to know when the Robinson family was in trouble or about to make a mistake? Well, I've never accepted the belief that being robot-like in golf would always lead to success. Sure, it's important to have a swing that you can repeat over and over, but as far as trying to *act* like a robot out on the golf course, I think it can be a serious mistake for a lot of people.

As I said earlier, golf is not a sport where the less expressive you are the better you'll be. Knowing your own personality, however, will lead to success. Look at golfers like Joanne Carner, Alison Nicholas and Dottie Pepper on the LPGA Tour, or Seve Ballesteros, Craig Stadler and Tiger Woods on the men's tour. You always know how they feel about a shot. Dottie and Allie and Tiger are a lot alike:

they'll use a little English to get their putts to roll right, or pump their fists when a long one drops in. Craig is like me when he misfires: you can see (and hear) him chastising himself. As for Joanne and Seve, there's no mistaking their pleasure when they stiff an approach or sink one for a birdie. They have two of the best smiles on tour.

In one way or another, I'm very much like all of these players. I'm emotional and passionate and I don't apologize for it. I also think it would be dangerous for me to try and be something I'm not. Which is just the point. You can't all of a sudden change who you are out on a golf course. You have to know yourself and know that your golf will be better if you are yourself. Some people express themselves better on paper, others in person.

It's the same thing in golf. All you have to do is realize that there are "different strokes for different folks." Part of the reason there are so many golf infomercials, gadgets and magazines out there is because no one thing works for everyone. In golf, as in life, there is no one right way. Some people are good at putting, others have a great short game and still others are at their best off the tee. You just have to know which one you are.

When I first started playing golf in Europe, I tried to be calm, cool and unemotional because I thought it would help my game. But one day Leo said to me, "God, you look like a zombie, like you're not enjoying what you're doing out there and you don't seem to care." He was right. I did feel like a zombie. I realized I needed to feel excited about what I was doing—and I needed to express it, too. So I began to let myself live all my shots a little bit more than the average golfer. I can't deny who I am and you shouldn't either.

Every golfer needs to find the intensity level that best fits them. Only then can you stay excited and stay in control. If you are a vocal person, a passionate person, then don't disown yourself out on the golf course. If you let yourself become too emotional it will no doubt hurt your game, but your golf will be affected even more negatively if you try to be something you're not. Similarly, if you are a laid-back kind of person, like Tammie Green or Annika Sorenstam, you shouldn't try to become a Dottie Pepper or an Alison Nicholas.

If you're an emotional player as I am, though, then sometimes you're bound to feel too intense out on the golf course. Perhaps there are times when you've felt irritated with every little shot. When that occurs you have to force yourself to get back to the right intensity level again. I don't care what kind of a personality you have—impulsive or mellow—everyone at one time or another loses their pace, their feel or their cool out on the course. The question is, what do you do about it?

I sometimes sing to myself—Counting Crows, Celine Dion, Amanda Marshall—in order to get back into my own mental groove. Anybody can do this. All you need to do is figure out what kind of music, whether it's Chopin or Smashing Pumpkins, helps you stay calm and relaxed and in the moment. Fuzzy Zoeller whistles while he's walking to his next shot and I've heard some golfers hum. Whatever gets you through the round.

Again, the reason it is important to know yourself is that it enables you to know how to help yourself out on the course. For instance, if you're someone who does not have a lot of confidence and has trouble recovering from difficult situations, then you need to recognize that you are probably someone whose enthusiasm can easily be quashed. Someone, perhaps, who is also easily persuaded to give up.

If that's the case, then directed daydreaming might help. Instead of feeling helpless if you're hitting it into the rough off every tee or missing close putts, visualize a different goal. Visualize the ball in the middle of the fairway before you hit your drive. Visualize the putt dropping before you start your stroke. If you are the kind of person who doubts yourself, then direct your thoughts and simply make them more positive.

On the other hand, if you're the kind of person, like me, who is tightly wound, then it's probably more important for you to take what I call mini-vacations. Let your energy work for you during your swing, but between times, while you wait for someone else to hit, let your mind go blank—focus on a tree in the distance, or a cloud or the color of your playing partner's shirt—and keep it simple. Then, when it's time for you to play, use your energy and concentration to get the ball to the hole, and if it drops, and it was a big putt, and you like to yell and scream as I do, by all means don't hold back.

5

Be the Ball

THE CONCENTRATION GAME

It's impossible to stay focused absolutely all of the time on the golf course. In fact, you shouldn't even try. That may sound like heresy, but it's true. To make the best use of your power of concentration, you have to know when to use it and when not to. Too much thinking, in general, can be bad for your golf game. Once you start saying to yourself, "Oh, I just made bogey, now I have to make a birdie," then you're in trouble. You've distracted yourself from the task at hand, and on top of it, you're now worried and stressed.

There are two keys to not going down this road. The first is to never think more than one stroke ahead. If you do, you're bound to lose your concentration and focus and your game will suffer. You shouldn't ever think about a birdie until you're actually putting for a birdie. The only thing you should be thinking about is making a good "next" shot. By thinking about all the other shots you want to make, you only end up exhausting yourself—playing a mental thirty-six holes instead of an actual eighteen. That's why professional golfers always talk about being in the present. You have no control over what you just did. And you have no control over what lies in front of you, either. The only thing you *do* have control over is your next shot.

The second key to staying focused is being decisive. And in order to be decisive, you must first consider your options: Where do you want your ball to go? What type of shot will get you there? And what club will enable you to make that shot? After considering the various possibilities, make your choices and, most important of all, stick to them. Try to time your pre-shot routine and keep it to a minimum. If you're exceeding forty-five seconds, you're probably taking too much time. Make your decision and execute. Questioning will only lead you to lose focus.

I should know. In the two years leading up to my hip surgery at the end of 1996, I was the poster child for "The Unfocused Golfer." I had injured myself years before in college when I crashed my bicycle after speeding (yeah, I know) down a steep hill. I never had an X ray, but it turns out I disconnected all the muscles in my right leg from the part of the hipbone that extends down into the buttocks area. The injury caused me to favor my right side and I became increasingly unbalanced in my swing. Up until the time I finally went to see a doctor about the old injury and had the surgery, I became more and more uncomfortable on the golf course. I was fidgety in my setup and I fiddled around continually, checking my alignment, my grip, my stance, my backswing. Absolutely everything. It took me forever to finally make a shot. I didn't trust anything I was doing and so I was never focused. Even when I would be walking to my next shot, I would have a club in my hand, trying to figure out what I was doing wrong. After twelve, thirteen holes, I felt mentally exhausted.

Since my surgery I've been able to return to being the feel player I really am, which means I don't think so much about what I'm doing when I'm out on the golf course. I just do it, and when I'm through with a shot, the club goes right back in the bag.

For most golfers, the less technical your thinking is when you're out on the course, the more energy you'll preserve for the actual execution of your golf shot. Staying focused is about keeping it simple. So think once (not twice) about what you want to do. Then lock and load and pull the trigger.

6

Whatever Gets You Through the Night

THE VALUE OF A DISTRACTION

No one, not even the best pros, can focus for four or five hours and expect to stay on top of everything. So to stay relaxed, when you're not actually over a shot you need to take a break. You need to give your brain a rest, to switch it off, because if you try to concentrate 100 percent of the time, you'll likely end up frying your brain. Do that and you'll not only lose whatever sharpness you had at the beginning of the round, but you'll find yourself completely stressed out.

Fanny Sunneson, Nick Faldo's caddy, once told me a good story about how she helped Nick to relax and to keep his mind off his game in between shots. It was during the last round of the 1994 British Open, when Nick won his second claret jug. As he and Fanny were walking the fairways of the back nine, Fanny would ask Nick about the new house he was building for his family. In between shots she pulled every question out of the bag that she could think of: did he like the new furniture; what wallpaper had Nick and his wife picked out, etc. All of this was a way to distract Nick from thinking too far ahead—which we all know is the golfer's curse—and to keep him relaxed.

Most of the time, we have to depend on ourselves to stay relaxed out on the course. I do a disappearing act. As soon as I hit my shot I "disappear" to a favorite beach in the Bahamas, order up a margarita or a piña colada and sip it as I walk down the fairway to my ball. By the time I start thinking about my next shot, I feel completely relaxed and comfortable (if not a bit tipsy!). When I arrive at my ball, I turn on the switch that allows me to focus on the next shot. While I've been walking up to my ball, I haven't wasted any energy thinking about the last shot or worrying about the next one.

But it is not always so easy to send yourself to the Bahamas. Sometimes when I'm not playing very well it's much harder to remain calm and relaxed and I can't reach the beach in my head at all. Before my surgery, it was as though I hadn't felt the sand beneath my feet in years. Instead, it was as if I was stuck in the traffic circle at the center of Paris going around and around the Arc d' Triomphe, without ever finding the way out.

There are so many things that are out of your control on the golf course that it becomes imperative to make the most of those things which *are* in your control—and one of them is what you think about between shots. If trying to imagine yourself on a beach in the Bahamas is too taxing, try looking around and taking in your surroundings, or even just chat up your playing partners. I seem to have a particularly good memory for off-color jokes, and at the very least, they seem to relax my partner, whether I'm paired with a fellow pro or a 12-handicapper in a pro-am. When I feel that my partner is relaxed, I feel more relaxed as well.

7

No Surrender

THE POWER OF POSITIVE THINKING

Like The Little Engine That Could, most of us start out thinking "we can't"—we doubt ourselves, second-guess ourselves, sometimes even, unwittingly, undermine ourselves.

One way we do this is by expecting too much from each shot. There's a real difference between saying to yourself, "Let's get this close to the pin" and saying, "I *need* to get this close to the pin." When we say the latter, we're really just setting ourselves up for failure. When we say we need something, we inject an air of desperation and put tremendous pressure on ourselves. Which is why something as seemingly innocuous as talking to yourself honestly can turn out to be beneficial to your play. Sure, getting close to the pin should be part of your planning: "I can do it; I'm going to do it." That's part of what it means to have a positive attitude. But be careful how you talk to yourself. As soon as you put "need" or "have to" in there, you are putting more pressure on yourself to perform, and the last thing anyone needs on a golf course is a little more performance anxiety!

When I shot that 63 in the 1994 U.S. Open, I hadn't expected to shoot the lights out that day. It was something that just happened. Every shot landed near the pin; every putt fell into the bottom of the cup. Then Saturday rolled around and somewhere in the middle of my round everything suddenly turned sour. Every shot landed in a bunker; every putt rolled past the cup. I couldn't figure it out. But what was worse, I started to "need" things to happen. I needed to hit fairways. I needed to get putts to drop. But the more I seemed to need things to happen, the less likely they were going to go my way. Patty Sheehan ended up winning and I ended up in ninth place. It was a painful experience, to be sure. In the same way that I couldn't figure out how I shot a 63, I couldn't figure out how I could suddenly lose so many strokes to par. But one thing I learned was certain: "needing" something on a golf course almost always sets you up for disappointment.

A positive attitude is different from "needing," and it isn't about fooling yourself, saying, "I feel great and oh, isn't my golf wonderful" when it's not. It isn't as simple as telling yourself that you can make every shot. That's dangerous thinking. You can't lie your way into a positive attitude when that's not how you're feeling or how you're playing.

But positive thinking requires confidence and confi-

BEING positive isn't about giving yourself an impossible task—"I'm going to win every tournament"—it's about the confidence that comes from *believing* in yourself.

dence shouldn't ever be about how you *do* something. It shouldn't depend on any exterior events or circumstances—like your last good round. Confidence should be about what's inside you. Your level of confidence shouldn't change drastically depending on how well—or badly—you play on any given day. If you usually shoot in the 90's, and then for a couple of days you can't seem to break 100, you shouldn't lose all of your confidence, thinking that your game has gone south and you're not going to get it back without some drastic adjustment.

Confidence comes from believing in yourself no matter what the situation. And no matter what the situation, you should always feel confident that you can find a way to succeed. One of the best ways to maintain your confidence is to rely on your memory. Every time you hit a good shot, you need to put it away in your memory bank. You should always be adding to it, never subtracting. When you make a particularly good shot on a difficult hole, or sink a long twisting putt, put the memory of what it felt like to swing the club or stroke the putter on those holes in your bank and then draw on those memories when you need to.

I always draw on the most recent good shot I made. (It gets tough when you go a while without making a good shot, but hopefully you don't have to go back too far.) The important thing to remember is that even when your game is inconsistent, you should work to make sure your confidence isn't.

Winning the next LPGA event after that disappointing Open was a hugely important moment for me. It taught me the value of not letting my confidence be broken by just one round, or by just one tournament, even if it was the U.S. Open. The key is staying faithful to yourself when you most want to run away.

8

It Don't Come Easy

THE VALUE OF REALITY TESTING

We all know golfers who cheat just a wee bit by kicking their ball into a better lie, or who shave a stroke or two off their score, just so they can feel better about their game. Women, it seems, don't have as much of a need to do this, so I think it's easier for us to be honest about how we're really playing. It also gives us a distinct advantage over men.

Sometimes life tests us to see how much we really want something. In order to get what we want, we have to be willing to be tough on ourselves. If I play really lousy one day I could blame it on everything else—on the course, the weather, the distractions of the crowd, my caddy, even my breakfast. But if you really want to be the best at anything you do, whether it's being the best salesperson or the best writer or the best 10-handicapper, you cannot lie to yourself, and you can't blame it on everything else.

Remember what it's like to be in love with the wrong

kind of guy? You know you shouldn't, but you just can't help yourself, and the more you tell yourself, "Oh, I'm not really in love with him," the more mixed up you seem to get?

Well, golf is no different. Whatever emotions you are having out on the course, you can't just deny them; you have to deal with them. No matter how crummy you may be feeling about your game on a particular day, you can always think about positive options. You can focus on what you need to do to just get the ball to the hole; on what clubs seem to be working best for you that day; on lining up your putts to give yourself a chance at par, or bogey, or double bogey.

But the most important attitude to bring to the golf course is a willingness to set your expectations at the right level. There are some days when you're happy with a 90. On other days you might not break 100, and you feel miserable. The important thing is to recognize that in both situations you can—you should—give 100 percent of your energy and focus.

Fellow Swede Anders Forsbrand, who played for a while on the PGA Tour, once told me a story about playing with an amateur who kept hitting the ball to the right, shot after shot. Finally, Anders suggested to the amateur that he might want to start by aiming more left since he knew he was pushing every shot. But the amateur just said, "How about if I hit it straight?" To me, that's a perfect example of not being honest with yourself. If the amateur was trying to make a specific correction, that's one thing, but in this case he just seemed to think that the ball would go straight "on the next shot." Most people do not hit the ball straight shot after shot. But if you *do* know where your shot is going every time, then there's no excuse not to set up to wherever that is.

The perfect swing is the one that produces the same result each and every time. Not everyone can come out of their spikes when they drive the ball the way Laura Davies does. And not everyone should try and duplicate the funky loop in Jim Furyk's swing. But each of those swings works for those golfers because they know what's comfortable for them and they know what their natural swing is. They are able to repeat that swing over and over again. I naturally set up a little right of the target. But before my hip surgery, when my swing was out of whack, I often set up a lot more to the right to try and compensate for the fact that I was hooking the ball a lot more.

Whether you hit it consistently right or consistently left, if you know where your ball is generally going to land, then you're ahead of the game. As far as having the perfect swing, forget it. Just be realistic about the swing you do have. You don't have to prove anything to anybody else as long as *you* know where your swing is going to take the ball.

9

Get Up, Stand Up

LEARNING FROM YOUR MISTAKES

In the movie *Steel Magnolias* one of the main characters says that she'd rather have a moment full of wonderful than a lifetime full of nothing. Most of us—from the 40-handicapper right down to the pros—play golf for the moments "full of wonderful" that it surprises us with. With amateurs those moments may be fewer and further between, but we all know what it's like, at one time or another, to hit the perfect drive, the perfect eight-iron, the perfect putt. And the reason we all continue to come out to the golf course is that we want to make *every* shot a moment full of wonderful. Reality, of course, tells us that most of our shots are not so wonderful.

No one has ever played an eighteen-hole round without wishing some shots back. A pedestrian shot or two will always pollute the most perfect of rounds, but it shouldn't prevent you from having the round of your life. The question is, what use can we make of our less-than-perfect shots?

Nearly everyone who teaches golf will tell you that what happened two seconds ago is history. Nothing can be done about it so you should deal with it and move on. We've all stopped in the middle of a round and asked ourselves, dejectedly, "Why?" But we usually ask this because we're mad at ourselves. We don't ask it because we really want to know why we play this game. If that were the case, we'd all turn into golfing Hamlets—tortured, indecisive and bound for deeper waters.

What most golf teachers don't often tell you is that it can be very useful to ask "Why?" after a round. I might even go so far as to say that a bad round is sometimes more useful to a golfer than a good one. Not that I'm ever happy about having a bad round, but in golf, as in life, you should be able to learn from your mistakes. No matter how good a golfer you are you need to always make adjustments. Golf is a game of fine-tuning, and sometimes hitting the ball badly points up more clearly what mistakes are being made and how they need to be remedied.

One of my favorite movies is *The Lion King,* and there's a scene in it, a joke between the young lion, Simba, and a monkey, that always hits home whenever I watch it. In the scene, Simba is sad about something and the monkey hauls off and hits him. Simba asks, "What did you do that for?" to which the monkey answers, "There's no use being sad, it's in the past and there's no changing it, only learning from it." So what happens, but about two seconds later Simba says something again about being sad. So, of course, the monkey takes another swing at the lion, but this time Simba ducks, at which point the monkey says, "See, you're learning from the past."

I've learned the hard way that worrying about someone else's game instead of keeping your head in your own can only lead to mistakes. At the 1993 Open I was leading at the start of the day. By the back nine, however, Lauri Merten was shooting a low score and had pulled ahead and I was a couple behind. I was very distracted, kept checking out the leader board, and in the end I missed a birdie putt on 18 that would have sent me into a playoff. I remember thinking, "Why did that happen? How did that happen?"

Sometimes it's hard to realize you're distracted when you're in the middle of being distracted. When I found myself leading going into the final round of the European Championship in Scotland last year, I reminded myself not to get caught up in what anyone else was doing. We were playing a tight golf course and I needed to really concentrate on my own game and just hit fairways and greens. You can only play your own game. You can't do anything about the other guy. Remembering that worked. I ended up pulling away and winning the tournament by five strokes.

We can't dwell in the past; we can't deny how we're feeling, but we can use it to our own advantage. And the only way to do that is to learn from our mistakes.

Takin' Care of Business

MAKING THE SHOT WHEN YOU NEED IT MOST

One thing that many women need more of out on the golf course is confidence. And to maintain confidence, women need to be more assertive. Now I don't mean for all you women golfers out there to suddenly announce to your male playing partners on the first tee that you're going to kick their collective butts. What I do mean is that you should believe in yourself, act with determination and never give in to the golf gremlins when they make you think you shouldn't be out there.

Part of believing in yourself is being in control of all the dozens of decisions you have to make during a round of golf, from club selection to shot-making strategy. Even when you're going for a double bogey, it's important that you feel comfortable and confident with the shot you're about to make. Remember, doubt is the number-one enemy in golf, so when you make a decision out there, stick with it. If I am addressing the ball and I am still wondering whether I have the right club in my hands, or whether the shot I'm going for is the one that will get me to the hole, how can I ever expect to make a good shot?

As long as you believe in your ability to make the shot you want, you're never out of the game. A few years ago I was playing in Germany in a European tour event called the Hennessey Cup. This is a tournament I've won twice, but on this particular day I was really struggling. I was either short of the green or over the green. Nothing seemed to be working for me and I felt as if I was fighting all day to make something happen and still coming up empty. I hit a good drive on the eighteenth hole, a par-5, and so I thought maybe I could give myself a chance for birdie by going for the green. Even at the conclusion of what was a very mediocre round, I was still trying to make something happen. Well, I slam-dunked my three-iron from a couple of hundred yards out for double eagle. In Europe we call a double eagle an albatross. However you describe it, it's rare; the most difficult (and perhaps the luckiest) shot in the book.

Then again, maybe it had nothing at all to do with luck. I'd put myself in a good frame of mind before that final shot and by doing so I really gave myself a chance not just for a birdie, but, as it turned out, for a double eagle. Staying aggressive, even when you're not playing the best round of your life, or even the second-best round of your life, is the real key to success. And it doesn't matter if you're being aggressive on the first shot of your round or the last, since as we all know, every shot counts in golf.

Being competitive and aggressive in sports doesn't always come as naturally to women as it does to men. Somehow men pick up that competitive attitude more quickly than women, or they're taught it earlier in life, or it's accepted more readily in them than in women—or all three. On the other hand, women are told, either implicitly or explicitly, that it is not feminine to be competitive, especially at a young age. This has already changed significantly in the past decade, but some attitudes really do die hard.

Similarly, there are numerous golf instructionals out there that still tell women they shouldn't try to overpower the ball. One of the subtle messages embedded in that idea is that women are inferior to men on the golf course. In other words, trying aggressive shots, like going for the green in two on a par-5 or using a two-iron to try and cut off a dogleg, is somehow "out of reach," literally and figuratively, for the female golfer.

It's no doubt true that women, in general, are not as strong as men and therefore they can't hit a golf ball as far. It's also true that women often accomplish with finesse the same goals in golf that men usually accomplish with raw power. But neither of those facts means women can't, or shouldn't, step up and play the game on their own terms— and let it rip.

I also think that young girls, not just women, should be

encouraged to let it all out on the competitive playing field, whether it's a golf course or a basketball court. Sure, it's important for young kids to experience the pure pleasure of sport before they're taught to go out and do everything they can to beat the opposing team or player. But what's wrong with letting girls, not just boys, know that it's okay to take the ball away from the other side, to score more points than the other team or to drive the ball farther than your partner?

Before you can score well, you have to *want* to score well. Then being more aggressive will make a difference in your golf game.

There are plenty of ways to bring out your own assertiveness on the course and I promise that they will help sharpen not only your competitive instincts, but your golfing skills as well.

For instance, have a driving competition on one of the par-5's with your playing partners. Or designate one of the par-3's for a closest-to-the-pin contest. You can put up a pot, or even designate a "poison" of choice—drinks, ice cream, whatever—to be bought by the player with the worst shot. A friendly wager has a way of getting the competitive juices flowing. If your playing partners are better golfers than you, ask them to spot you a stroke a hole to level the playing field. Invent your own skins game. Even at 50 cents a hole, the entire round can suddenly seem more exciting. Better yet, making bets can help sharpen your skills because you'll find yourself focusing more on every shot. Too many times we get into situations where our level of care and concentration is lower than it should be.

Even when you're playing alone you can challenge yourself to be more aggressive. If you hit a good drive, for example, then try to hit the next one even farther. Or tee it up from the blue tees. Or count up how many greens you hit in your last round and try to hit more next time. We make goals all the time whether we are working, raising a family or both; so you should make a goal every time you go out and play a round of golf. Heck, as women we've been setting tasks for ourselves ever since the Garden of Eden when Eve made a mental note to herself: "Give apple to Adam"!

Swing Time

LEGS ARE A GIRL'S BEST FRIEND

Sooo, now that I've got your head in order, let's get your swing in gear, too.

There are an awful lot of things about golf that seem counterintuitive. One of them, certainly, is the belief that the harder you swing the farther your ball will go. We all want to hit the golf ball a mile, so we often grip the club tighter, swing higher and faster . . . and top the ball about fifty yards. When we swing harder we usually end up making two fatal mistakes: we swing up and we swing with our arms. Nothing will kill a good round quicker than those two things.

Imagine standing perfectly still and trying to throw a javelin or a baseball with just your arm. Neither would go very far. Same thing with a golf club. Swing with just your arms and the ball goes about thirty yards. The arms are powerless without the support of the body behind them.

Women who are self-conscious about their game make this mistake frequently. In an effort to stay in control, they don't incorporate their entire body into the swing. By and large, women are too tentative in their ball striking, too afraid of hitting the ball into the ground, and it shows because more often than not they top the ball or hit it thin.

But when women do try to hit the ball harder, they usually use their arms too much. And because they are trying so hard to get their arms around in the swing, and get under the ball to try and lift it up, they tend to have too much movement in their lower body. Too much movement in the body results in the club going too far back and a lot of energy is wasted in the downswing.

For women, especially, who want to hit the ball with more power, there are two essential things to always keep in mind.

1) Maintaining a low center of gravity.

2) Keeping the club away from the body on the backswing.

First things first. Your balance is in your stance and your center of gravity is in the middle of that stance—in your stomach and your buttocks. You might be wincing at this news—the last thing you want to think about when you're out playing golf is your body—but it's not about how you look, it's about how you set up to the ball. If your parents were the type who were always scolding you to stand up straight, count your blessings. Golf is about posture.

Like baseball, rowing and a lot of other sports, golf seems to require great arm strength. But it's not the arms that are most important in golf, it's the legs. This is good news, since women's legs are almost as strong as men's, and much stronger than women's arms. The reason our legs are so important in golf is because most of the power generated in the swing comes from a stable and well-balanced center of gravity. Again, that center is located primarily in our buttocks, and this is where we get the support—the stable base—for our golf swing. The stronger and more stable our lower body, the better chance we have to generate the centrifugal force that powers that tiny little white sphere through the air.

A stable lower body will generate more speed, more torque in the swing and thus more power. Women often center their gravity too high and thus have less balance when they swing. The lower you can get your center of gravity the better. If you are a tall person like me, and you have long legs, you need to bend your knees a bit more at the address, make sure your feet are as far apart as your shoulder blades and stick your butt out a bit more so that your center is as low as possible.

For women with shorter legs, you don't need to bend your knees as much in order to lower your center of gravity—you're already closer to the ground. Once you've centered yourself with your stomach and your buttocks, you're almost ready to start your swing.

Now forget everything I've said about how unimportant

WHEN you set up to the ball, make sure your head is over your feet, not behind them. Flex your knees and keep the flex the same throughout your swing. If you do, your hips will stay level too.

the arms are. The arms alone cannot generate power, but with a stable body in place the arms can deliver the centrifugal force needed to launch your ball—as long as you keep those arms away from your body.

Did you ever play tetherball growing up? That's the game where you use your hands to swat at a rubber ball that's attached by a long string to the top of a stationary pole. Imagine that that pole is like your lower body: a stable, balanced center of gravity. If I'm holding the tetherball and I want to whip it hard around the pole, I start way on the outside and throw it around in a high, wide arc. The tetherball moves faster that way because it gathers more centrifugal force. It's the same with the golf club. The more of an arc—the farther away from my body the clubhead is—the greater the centrifugal force generated by the swing.

Think about keeping your front arm straight through the backswing. When you get to the top of your swing that front arm will bend slightly. That's okay. Your arm will straighten out on the downswing. At impact you want to have both your arms fully extended and away from your body to maximize power.

Take a look at the example par excellence: Tiger Woods. Tiger's power, first of all, comes mostly from his legs, even though he moves them very little in his backswing. But the width of his swing is crucial to the distance he's able to get on his drives. Tiger's ability to keep the club away from his body means that he generates a tremendous amount of centrifugal force. And when all that force meets the ball on impact . . . well, you know what happens next. I'm not suggesting that we can all hit like Tiger Woods. But you can hit more like Tiger if you remember to keep a low center of gravity and keep your arms away from your body on the backswing.

Hard Habit to Break

KNOW YOUR RIGHT SIDE,
BUT DON'T OVERDO IT

David Feherty, the Irish pro who is now a golf commentator, once told me a very funny story about playing in a proam early in his career. His amateur partner hit his ball into a sand trap and was faced with a particularly awkward wedge shot. The amateur tried to lob the ball onto the green, but instead he hit it straight up in the air. When the ball came down it hit the golfer on his head, then bounced into his front shirt pocket! The amateur didn't have a clue as to what rule should apply for his next shot, so David jumped in and suggested that he bend over to retie his shoes—while standing next to the flag.

Other than being pretty funny, this story illustrates something that a lot of amateurs—and in particular women—have a tendency to do, which is to swing up on the ball. The reason golfers do this is that they think they have to help the ball up into the air, so instead of hitting down on the ball (which is the proper angle of attack), they get too much under it and scoop it. The result is that the ball simply pops up.

The best way to prevent this from happening is to set up for the shot with the proper backswing. Women need to think about hitting down on the ball and accelerating through the downswing.

If you're right-handed, the right side of the body is where the power comes from and you shouldn't be afraid to use it. When you begin your backswing your hips should rotate directly under your arms as they are going back. Make sure to keep the hips horizontal and on a level plane as your arms go up on your backswing. When you feel your left shoulder under your chin, you should be at the top of your swing. Most of your weight should be on the right knee, which should be slightly bent.

One test to make sure you're swinging on a level plane is to think about keeping your head on the same level at all times. Imagine you are swinging inside a box that is exactly the same height as you are and is just big enough to accommodate the perfect swing. Imagine also that there is a shelf running right under your chin. If your head hits the top of the box when you swing, you know you're coming up and not staying level. Chances are you'll then top the ball. Likewise, if your chin hits that shelf, you're probably dipping, and therefore hitting the ball fat.

Another problem that a lot of women—and men, for

AT the top of the backswing, your left shoulder should be under your chin. This will help you return to the starting position. Notice, also, that at the top of the backswing my club is just short of parallel. The biggest misconception people have about generating power is that you need to have a huge backswing. You don't. A solid position in the backswing is what you need most to fire in the downswing.

that matter—tend to bring on themselves is swinging past parallel for more power. Most people think that the longer your swing is, the more power you'll generate. Nope. It may seem counterintuitive, but I guarantee that the less backswing you have, the more power you'll be able to deliver to the ball. Let me explain.

When you let your club go past parallel at the top of the swing, the weight of the clubhead drops below your hands. All of a sudden you have a lot of gravity pulling on the clubhead. It becomes heavy, and most people, unless they have the strength of a John Daly, will try to counter all this weight by uncocking the wrists way too soon on the backswing. Now you're trying desperately to get the clubhead down fast and instead you get the shoulders, arms and hands moving too early. Whatever power you were hoping to generate with that extra-long swing you've now completely squandered.

Get Back

THE POWER IN STAYING BEHIND THE BALL

If the sexiest thing in golf is the big drive, then the downswing is a lot like foreplay. It's all about timing. You should begin the downswing by moving your left knee very slightly toward the target. This will help you start unwinding your lower body first, staying behind the ball, and put you in perfect position for the power shot. When the left knee moves first, the hips should follow, and then the shoulders. The arms and the clubhead will then automatically catch up, insuring a power-producing weight shift. Also, the quicker you turn your hips and the quicker you can bring your right side down to the ball, the more power you'll generate.

The most important thing about the downswing is not to unwind your upper body too early. Many amateurs make this mistake. The problem with unwinding with your shoulders and upper body too quickly is that you come over the top. What this means is that you're swinging the club outside in, resulting in either a hook, or more often, a huge slice.

This is what you should think about when swinging for power: First, when in address make sure your feet are apart at about the same width as your shoulders. The farther apart your feet, the more stable a base you have to work from. Your knees should be flexed, your backside out, your shoulder and neck muscles relaxed. With your legs flexed, your kneecaps should be directly over the balls of your feet. You don't want to have your weight back on your heels, because that will cause you to lose your balance when you try to swing.

Keeping in mind that it is not necessary to have a long backswing to hit a long ball, turn your shoulders so that your left shoulder ends up under your chin and pointing directly down at the ball. This should set you up perfectly at the top so that your left arm is exactly perpendicular to the club shaft. Instead of overswinging past parallel, where your hand would be at twelve o'clock above your head, the shorter backswing means your hands should be more or less in an eleven o'clock position above your head. This way you also avoid flexing your left wrist too much at the top of your swing. Again, if you let your left wrist bend too much you'll allow the clubhead to dip below the hands. When that happens the power that should come from your downswing will be compromised—your arms will move before your right side and the proper power sequence—torso, arms, hands and club—will be lost.

Another advantage to the shorter backswing is that your hips should naturally turn about half as much as your shoulders. More hip turn than that and you'll probably lose your balance a bit and feel forced to move your upper body too soon. By limiting your hip turn, you'll give yourself a better chance of starting your downswing properly, with your lower body first. At waist-high in the downswing, the club should again be at a right angle to your left arm. This is the prime ball-striking position and exactly the correct preparation for a powerful hit. With the hips not having to rotate back to the left side too much, your weight should still be centered on the inside of your left foot. The hips rotating back to the left side allows the club to drop on the perfect inside plane, the upper body remaining behind the ball, and the lower body clearing the way for a strong release.

The other element to the swing that will maximize power is keeping your arms away from your body in order to give your swing more of an arc. Remember, the farther the clubhead is away from you, the greater the radius of your swing, the more centrifugal force (that is, power) you'll be able to generate.

You often hear about a piece of instructional advice called the "flying elbow," about not letting the right arm get too far away from the body at the top of the swing. Amateurs

DURING the swing you want to keep everything moving together. Your arms should always be extended and your hands should always be to the right of your head. Also, keeping your club at a right angle to your wrists and arms will put you in the power position at impact.

HERE I'm in the perfect position at the moment of impact. My upper body is behind the ball. My hands are slightly forward. And my legs are driving through the ball. All these elements are crucial for finishing off a powerful swing.

often overcompensate for this by tucking the right elbow into the body too much, thereby decreasing the power potential in the downswing.

Instead, during the backswing you should think about allowing your right arm to come away from your side. In fact, at the top of your backswing your right arm should be bent at a ninety-degree angle at the elbow. What this does is enable you to keep your left arm straight and at the same time it creates a natural, wide arc to the backswing. From this position, your right arm should then move freely toward your body during the downswing, creating additional leverage and therefore more clubhead speed.

Get a Grip

KNUCKLE UP, NOT UNDER

It is my experience when giving clinics and playing in pro-ams that most women don't use a strong enough grip. They tend to get underneath the club, grasping it more with their palms. When you grip the club more on the top with your left hand the ensuing swing will result in more power. But a stronger grip is harder to maintain, because it takes more strength to roll your hands over through the downswing.

Most women don't have especially fast hands, like a Tiger Woods or a Kelly Robbins. So the best way to use a stronger grip to insure that you roll your hands over on the downswing is to knuckle up. With your left hand, grip up two or three knuckles onto the shaft. Your left hand should be closed over the grip of the club so that at least the first knuckle of your index finger is on top of the shaft and the "V" created by your left hand should point toward your left shoulder.

IF you want to hit for power, I advise a stronger grip than usual for women. This means a stronger left hand. You should show two knuckles as my grip does here, with your left thumb just right of the center of the club. Anything less than two knuckles will mean more work for your wrists. A stronger grip allows you to let the club swing through to release more easily.

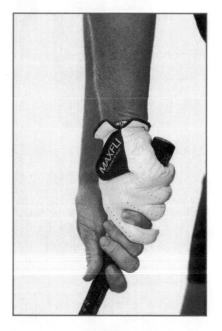

THERE are three different kinds of grip: the interlocking grip (shown here); the baseball grip; and the overlapping grip. I have small hands like a lot of women and so the interlocking grip for me is a more secure way to hold the club.

One warning. Taking a strong grip does *not* mean gripping the club with more pressure. Gripping your club too tightly will produce tension in your arms and shoulders that will reduce the power of the swing.

We often don't know that we're gripping the club too tightly, usually in an attempt to maintain control of the club. You want to maintain a constant grip pressure throughout the entire swing. One way to figure out what the right grip pressure should be is to imagine you're holding a roll of cookie dough, the kind you used to eat right out of the package with your high school friends. (And then felt ill afterward.) Well, imagine the grip of your club as the roll of cookie dough. You want to press it firmly enough so that you can indent it with each of your fingers, but not so firmly that you squeeze the roll so it changes shape. Your hands should feel at ease, but in control of the club.

The Rhythm Method

SLOWER IS BETTER

Timing, as we all know, is everything in life. And finding your own rhythm is critical in creating the swing that's right for you.

One way to do this is to go out and practice some gentle chip shots without using your arms too much, but rather your whole body. A slower, more abbreviated swing will usually imitate the proper sequence of body movements you need in the full swing. Think about each particular body movement and how it fits into your swing. No matter how fast the club goes, your body should follow the movements in the slower swing.

Most women are very surprised when they learn the half shot usually sends the ball farther than their full swing does. The reason is that they are more likely to use their whole body when taking an easy swing and they're not trying to overpower the ball. When you use your lower body—everybody say it with me—your swing will naturally be more powerful.

In practicing that half shot, limit your backswing to the nine o'clock position and your follow-through to the three o'clock position, just like a pendulum. Swing up and down very slowly. I call this the "grandma" swing, but it helps you to get the feel for how the different parts of your body should all be working together in the swing. Put the club handle in your belly button and try swinging from there, and feel how your swing goes with your body as it turns back and then forward again. You should feel a kind of natural rhythm here and a connection between your arms and your legs.

Once you feel comfortable with the rhythm of the swing, it's time to figure out exactly how far you can hit the ball. The techniques I've discussed so far are all meant to maximize the power in the perfect swing. But what if you don't have a "perfect" swing? There are several ways for you to figure out how far you can hit the ball and what the best swing is for your particular abilities.

First of all, you need to think about stepping into the ball, the way a baseball player at bat does when he shifts from his back foot to his front. Ballplayers, just like golfers, don't hit the ball with their arms, but with the support of their body. The key is timing, and if you can coordinate your body and your arms together at impact, you can't help but hit the ball with power.

With that in mind, go out and try to hit the ball as hard as you can—not with your arms, but with your lower body. See how hard you can hit the ball while still maintaining at least some coordination and control between your body and your arms. This exercise should show you the limits of your swing, how hard you can swing while still maintaining control.

The next thing to figure out is the limit of your hip turn. Again, the ideal turn is about forty-five degrees. Anything more than that and it will take too long for your arms to catch up on the downswing. A lot of women can't turn a full forty-five degrees, but this should not discourage them. They can still generate a lot of power from their lower bodies.

Stand in front of a mirror, touch the end of the club to your belly button and turn to the right, still holding the club out from your stomach. When you start to feel that you can't turn your hips any farther without using your arms, that's what your hip turn should look like. In this exercise, your body is actually telling you how far you are able to turn in the backswing. One way of cheating is to let your left foot come up just a little bit in order to extend the hip turn. You see professional golfers doing this all the time when they play. When the turn starts to feel uncomfortable then you know the limit of your hip turn.

THIS is a good exercise to make sure
you are keeping your hips in the
proper position throughout the turn.
Put the grip end of your club on
your belly button and hold the club
in the middle, pointing it straight out
in front of you. As you turn, the club
should stay on a parallel plane. Try to
memorize the position of your hips
as you do this. If the club comes up,
you're not turning your hips and
stomach enough.

Remember to keep your head and shoulders on the same plane. Your shoulders, too, need to open and close on the same level. The golf swing should be like opening and closing a door. If the hinges aren't straight, the door won't open properly.

How to Stay on the Straight and Narrow

AND AVOID GOING OVER THE TOP

Variation on an old joke: How do you get to the U.S. Open? Practice, practice, practice. A friend of mine on tour, Dale Reid, used to practice all the time as a teenager growing up in Scotland. Because Dale didn't have a lot of money to buy her own balls, she'd go to a local driving range and, camouflaged as a bush, would inch her way out onto the back of the range and fill up her pockets.

Most of the professional golfers I know practice their craft quite a bit. Some of them, like Joanne Carner and Nick Faldo, are legendary for it. Joanne, for instance, has been known to hit balls for six hours at a time.

You may not be as dedicated to practicing as Dale or Joanne, but if you practice at all, one of the most important things to work on is the downswing. A flatter swing plane (where the club is more behind your head than over it at the top) goes hand in hand with a strong grip. At the top of the swing your hands should be very close to the level of your right shoulder. By swinging on a flatter plane your hands will automatically bring your club onto a more inside path as you start the downswing. The result is that as you follow through you'll swing the clubhead out more directly toward the target.

One of the most common problems in any amateur's swing occurs at the beginning of the downswing when, instead of taking an inside-out path, they take the club "over the top." What that means is that they are throwing the club out too far and away from the body on the downswing instead of drawing it in. The reason for this is because they're unwinding with their arms and shoulders too soon.

The out-to-in path that the club takes when you go over the top means you never get on the target line and you end up swiping at the ball instead of hitting it solid. If your club face is open at impact, you'll slice the ball. If it's closed or to the left of the target, you'll pull the ball. Take my word for it, I had to suffer through way too many hooks and slices before I had the surgery that reattached my right hamstring to my hipbone. Because of the injury, I didn't have the strength to keep my clubhead inside the target line on the downswing and so I played a lot of "army" golf—right, left, right, left— and learned more about forestry than I cared to know.

For those of you who have just gotten stuck in the over-the-top habit, there is a cure. First off, you've probably gotten yourself into the over-the-top dilemma because you're swaying too much, instead of turning your hips during the backswing. When that happens you find yourself so far back on your right side that it's almost impossible to shift back to your left on the downswing. Instead, what happens is that you hang back on your right side and perform the downswing entirely with your arms and shoulders, killing whatever power you thought you were generating. At the same time, the early rotation of your shoulders means you've carried your arms and club out to the right, away from your body, and unfortunately in perfect position for a drive-killing, outside-to-in swing. Not only have you lost all power in your swing, but the ball is now going to go either left or right depending on how open or closed your club face is at impact.

So, instead of sliding in your backswing and having too much movement in your lower body, keep your legs quiet and concentrate on turning your shoulders and hips. This will set up the proper sequence (legs, hips, shoulders, arms, club) when you start to unwind on the downswing and insure that you'll still deliver all that centrifugal force to the ball.

The other fringe benefit of moving your lower body toward the target first on the downswing when you begin to unwind your hips is that your arms and your club will naturally drop in nearer to your body. In this way, you can attack the target line more directly and cut down on your chances of slicing or pulling the ball. With most of your weight now on your left leg and foot at impact, you will soon see the result of having put yourself in a powerful ball-striking position.

Hint: Make sure that after you tee the ball up, you set up so that your left foot is slightly open and your left heel is on the same horizontal plane as the ball. You can use your left shoulder, too, to confirm your setup (if you're right-handed), since the ball should be just inside a point below that shoulder. If you place the ball too far forward in your stance, you're setting yourself up for an outside-in path because you will find yourself rotating your right shoulder outward in order to get the clubhead back behind the ball. So before you even have to think about your swing, make sure you don't tee the ball up too far forward in your stance.

Hint: Most golfers have a tendency to take too many practice swings. Don't. It only ends up tiring you out. A practice swing should be like an intended shot. In other words, it should simulate what you actually want to do. You can also take too many practice putting strokes. Believe it or not, they can tire you out too. And the real danger of becoming tired is that you lose your focus. It's best to take one full practice swing, and then to set yourself up in the stance to hit. Take your club back a yard so your arms groove into your intended swing, and then bring the clubhead down to where you want to impact the ball. That way you can see and feel the position you want your body to be in when you actually swing through the ball. After that . . . play away!

The One True Thing

Hitting the ball properly is only part of getting the ball to your intended target. The other half is aiming.

First, think about where you want to hit the ball—and not about where you don't want to hit the ball. A coach of mine back in Sweden always walked the course with me before I played and pointed out places where I should aim: what side of the fairway, what part of the green, etc. He never pointed out the places I should stay away from because that would create fear in my mind. Proper visualization, he taught me, is about positive thinking.

Second, remember aiming is something a golfer has to do before he even sets up to the ball. An archer will never let go of his arrow before he aims it at the target he wants to hit. The same goes for the golfer. In order to get to the target you want to hit, you need to line up three things: your body, your ball and the target you're aiming at.

The initial thing you should do to get your body aimed properly is to locate the intended target and then make a mental photo of it you can refer to when you're setting up on the ball. In fact, you want to be able to see the target in your head and you want to feel where it is in your body. This may seem like a strange thing to say, but it's not. Having a sense or feeling of where the target is allows your body to adjust accordingly. Professional golfers do this without even thinking, but anyone who plays golf regularly can do it as well. Did you ever play when it was getting very dark outside? That can be a good time to test your ability to feel for the target. I know golfers who have finished rounds in complete darkness, without missing a fairway or green, because they could feel where the pin was.

Whatever the target you've picked out, the last thing in your head before you start your swing should be the mental picture of that target. If you're swinging correctly your body will automatically follow your thoughts and move in the direction of the target. Think about throwing a ball. You always look at the other person before you throw it—you look at the target—and the way you follow through with your leg and arm motion is in the direction of that other person. Your body moves naturally toward whatever you're aiming at.

Visualizing a shot helps you figure out how you're going to play a hole. You start by finding your target and thinking backward: "How do I get there and what do I need to do to get my ball to that place?'' You should consider distance, obstacles, conditions and club selection. Do you want to hit a high, arcing shot or a straight shot that will roll for thirty more yards? Try to imagine the shape of the shot you want to hit. Then, when you finally settle over the ball and place your club behind it to pre-aim the shot, you should feel confident that you've made the right choices to get your ball to the target.

You've probably seen professional golfers on TV go behind their ball to aim it down the fairway. Many of them extend their club out toward the target they are aiming at to get a sense of the line. While they're doing this they are checking for an intermediate target as well. An intermediate target is only three or four feet in front of ball, instead of 150 or 250 yards in front.

By picking an intermediate target in the grass just ahead of your ball, you make lining up your shot that much easier, because once you're addressing the ball, you are looking out at your target from a skewed position. By focusing on that spot in the grass you picked out when you stood behind your ball, you'll stay on line when you stand over the ball.

Aiming your putts is the same as aiming your drives. You never want to pick your line when you're in address, only when you are standing behind the ball and have the correct perspective. And in just the same way that you pick an intermediate target when you are driving, you should pick an intermediate point over which you want your ball to roll on its way to the hole. When you get to the green, mark your ball and then replace it with the brand label pointing along the intended line. The last thing you should look at before making your putt is the intermediate target. The only reason to look at the hole itself is in order to gauge the speed of the putt.

Hint: Your hands should always be very relaxed on the putter, and you should always make sure that the back side of your left hand stays strong to the target and doesn't pull up. An even tempo and a smooth swing should define your putting stroke the same way they define your regular swing.

Feel, Trust, Deliver

THE PRE-SHOT ROUTINE

Consistency and preparation mean everything in golf, so having a routine that you can repeat over and over before each shot is just as important as training your muscles to repeat certain actions over and over. A pre-shot routine helps you build a kind of cocoon around yourself as you're preparing to hit your next shot. This is the time when you very much want to be in the "zone" that all athletes refer to longingly. Really, though, there's nothing mysterious about it. When you sit and read a magazine—say a really juicy story in *People*—and you become so involved in it that you don't hear when the person sitting next to you asks you a question, that's being in the zone. In golf, you want to get in the same kind of zone over every shot. Essentially, you're thinking about what you want to do with the ball and where you want it to go. There should be no room for distraction or interference.

In order to figure out the best pre-shot routine, you first need to figure out about how long it takes for you to set yourself up for the shot. You don't want to take too long and fidget too much; that only gives you more time to lose your focus.

One of my failures in the past few years was not having any pre-shot routine. With my injury I was always looking for a way to compensate, constantly tweaking my swing even when I was about to hit a shot! When you become as uncomfortable as I was with my setup, there is no way you're going to feel you are making good decisions out there. And if you don't feel right from the start, how the hell are you going to feel right anywhere along the path of the golf swing? At the end of the 1996 season I could stand and look at the target, but I felt no connection between myself and the place I was supposedly aiming at. In fact, I had no idea how the ball was going to end up at the target. This was primarily because I hadn't worked out a swing that felt comfortable and I wasn't confident that the one I had was going to get the ball from "here" to "there."

Now that I am healthy again, I'm back to being a feel player, trusting my swing and the pictures in my head. My pre-shot routine is also much quicker. Many golfers squander too much time before taking their shot. Again, you do yourself a disservice when you take too long, because you usually lose your focus. It's helpful if you can get somebody to time you from the moment you get to your ball until you start your swing. Ideally, I think you should take no more than eight or nine seconds to take a practice swing, line up your target, stand over the ball and take a short pre-swing waggle to see where you want to be at impact before pulling the trigger. If you are taking thirteen, fourteen, fifteen seconds, you're probably taking too much time. Try timing yourself to see what feels most comfortable. You don't want to hurry your swing, but again, remember you want to maintain your sharpness and not allow yourself time to be distracted.

The main elements of the pre-shot routine are:

1) Sighting your target and figuring out what's needed to get the ball there.

2) Taking a full practice swing.

3) Finding your intermediate target as you stand behind the ball.

4) Picturing the target as you stand in address.

5) Taking a final one quarter practice swing to see how you should feel at impact.

6) Settling over the ball with the target in your mind.

When I think of my own pre-shot routine, I think of three very important words: feel, trust and deliver. You want to feel right over the ball before you're ready to swing. And when you do feel right, when you feel the target pulling at you, you can trust that you have what it takes to make the shot. When you trust yourself, you are then ready to deliver your golf shot. Without feel, there's no trust, and without trust, you have no way on earth of knowing if you are going to get the ball to the target. As much as people talk about technique in golf, a lot of what we all do comes down to having the right feeling. Without that, we're essentially at sea.

The Option Plan

HOW TO THINK YOUR WAY AROUND THE COURSE

An often overlooked aspect of good golf is that the more options you have, the better off you are. You don't ever want to think that you have only one shot that will get the ball to the hole. Just because you have only fourteen clubs in your bag doesn't mean you have only fourteen shots. You should be able to make at least three or four different kinds of shots with each of your clubs, and often more. As an amateur you probably don't have time to perfect even half of all those shots, but it's important to learn that there are many more kinds of shots than there are clubs in your bag.

Knowing that you have many options gives you a tremendous sense of control over your game. It also keeps the game interesting! Seve Ballesteros is someone I've always admired for his shot-making skills. His strength comes in knowing that no matter where he is he can always get himself out of trouble. He has mastered every lie and won tournaments not by hitting fairways every time, but by having a shot for wherever he found his ball—or at least an idea of how to play that shot. There are too many pros today who don't have that kind of repertoire and who when they suddenly find themselves off the fairway don't have a clue as to how to get out of trouble. Seve is a consummate player because he gets a whole lot more out of his fourteen clubs than just fourteen shots.

When I won the British Open in 1990 I was hooking it up on the green on one hole, fading it up there on another, then hitting a low running shot to the green on the next. It was a terrific feeling because I was able to see all the different shots I needed to make. It felt as though I had at least thirty clubs in my bag!

Of course, before you can think about what shots you are capable of playing, you need to know how the ball reacts to your particular swing. Sometimes I think the best golf teacher is the golf ball. You should learn the parameters of ball flight, how it hooks and slices, pulls, draws and fades, so that you know exactly what you can do with the ball when you need to do something other than hitting it straight.

Most people have a natural fade or draw to their swing. For most women, including myself, it's usually a draw, so knowing that, you'll want to aim to the right of your target. By aiming to the right, your natural draw will bring the ball back into the middle of the fairway. But if you don't know if your swing has a tendency to fade or draw, you're at a disadvantage. Knowing your swing and what the ball does naturally when you hit it means you'll have more confidence about where to aim the ball.

I have what I like to call a "spare bag" of shots. Not everyone wakes up feeling as if they're going to crush the ball that day. More often than not, we realize pretty quickly that it's going to be a struggle just to stay alive out there. When this happens, sometimes the best thing to do is choke down on your clubs and hit half shots that will steady a shaky swing and give you more confidence. By doing this, you create a kind of "comfort zone" for yourself. You also give yourself more options. Often we get so hooked up in hitting the perfect shot that we forget how helpful it can be to experiment with "safety" shots—shots to get you out of trouble when you're not feeling at your peak. Phil Mickelson is the kind of golfer who loves to practice all different kinds of shots. He likes to see how high the ball goes if he plays a shot one way, or how far it will go if he plays it another. Mickelson is one of the greatest short game players in golf precisely because he has so many different shots. He could lob a golf ball off a billiard table and still get it close to the hole.

One way to practice taking different kinds of shots is to make a game out of it. Children often challenge each other to see who can throw a ball over a tall tree or through an open window. You can challenge your partners to a closest-to-the-pin contest—maybe even with eyes closed. It can also

IN the follow-through, you want to have everything pointing toward the target. Notice my head has followed through with my swing and I'm looking at the target. My belly button, and therefore my hips, are facing in that direction. And my right foot, heel off the ground, is turned toward the target as well.

help to try some impossible shots, just to see what happens, like trying a two-iron out of a bunker. When I was a kid we had special tournaments where we could only play with two or three clubs. I remember having to use a driver on a short par-3. It tested the imagination, but it increased my repertoire. I know I can putt with a sand wedge if my ball is backed up against the fringe. Or I can hit a full wedge fifty yards if I need to get up and over a huge tree. Or I can fade the ball around an obstruction. Having these shots "in my bag" means that I don't have to worry about problems that ordinarily would have made me angry and anxious. But some things never change: chances are I'll still be fairly expressive about the situation!

Now when I find my ball behind a disgustingly huge tree, instead of thinking the only way I'm going to get the ball around it is to use an ax, I say to myself, "Okay, that's not so bad, all I have to do is decide which side of the tree I should take the ball around." If you can see a shot, you can hit a shot, but rarely do we practice the shots we'd rather not have to make. Practicing the perfect shot isn't nearly as helpful as practicing for a difficult shot.

Did You Ever Have to Make Up Your Mind?

PLAYING THE PERCENTAGES

Part of the reason for making sure you have a spare bag of shots is so you can then calculate what is the best shot for the best situation. To do that you have to know what your best shots are and what you feel capable of doing during that round. If I'm not hitting my driver well and I find myself on a par-5 with an open fairway, I might use my three-iron instead. Or you can't possibly get the ball onto the green in regulation unless you use a three-wood out of the short rough, only you haven't hit your three-wood all day. What should you do? Knowing that you'll probably end up in more trouble if you use your three-wood, you decide to swallow your pride and use a club that will get you out of the rough but not all the way back to the green. Or you realize you won't be able to make it across the water on a long par-3, so you decide to lay up or go for the neck of the fairway that curves around the water to the green. Perhaps you know that your five-iron will just barely get you over the water. Instead, take out a four-iron and shoot for a safe place behind the green. The point here is to always look for the safe shot instead of going for it and trying to hit the perfect shot when you know that if you're just a little off you'll end up in deep trouble.

You will always give yourself a lot more room to maneuver if you know when the percentages are against you. The important thing is to take out a club you feel comfortable with and play it safe, even if that means taking the less direct route to the hole. Know your capabilities and plan accordingly. Don't be greedy.

In fact, you should always have a plan going into each and every hole—a plan that you will probably have to keep revising as you go—so that you can feel confident that you're playing the club and the shot you really want. This is what is meant by "playing to your strength." Sometimes it even helps to play backward in your mind. Ask yourself what club you would like to hit to the green. By knowing what your best club is and what your best shot is, you will maximize your chances for success.

My advice for all golfers who shoot in the 90's or higher is to never hit your irons as hard as you can. Instead, go one club more. The reason is that if you have a flaw in your swing, the harder you swing, the more glaring that fault is going to be. If you think you need to crank a seven-iron, take a six instead. Choke down on it and swing a little easier and you'll probably get the same distance you thought you'd get from the seven, only without the flaws. Likewise, why use a full wedge when you can chip a nine-iron onto the green and swing a bit easier doing it?

Remember, golf is not about vanity. Too many men, for instance, take it as a matter of pride that they use certain clubs, like the driver, or that they can hit a five-iron 225 yards. But all that is wasted energy if you can't really get the ball to the hole in an efficient way. So know your swing and know your own power; and manage yourself around the golf course accordingly. Also, be aware of what clubs you may be hitting particularly well during your round and which ones you're not. Your score will suffer if you use a driver when you should be using your three-wood instead.

Of Shafts and Sweet Spots

CHOOSING THE RIGHT EQUIPMENT

Today, golf manufacturers are aiming more and more at women when it comes to designing woods with more flexible shafts and bigger sweet spots. Women should take advantage of the new golf technology. It's one more way of leveling the playing field.

A lot of women on the LPGA Tour are carrying more woods in their bags than ever before. Obviously, for women looking to increase the distance on their drives, this is a good route to go, and with today's new club designs, there's no excuse anymore for a woman to complain that she's not strong enough to hit the ball with her woods. Women should carry a driver, a five-wood and/or a seven-wood, even a nine-wood. Liselotte Neumann, who is a top player on the LPGA Tour, carries five woods in her bag.

The advantage of having these extra woods is that they can take the place of your long irons, which are difficult to control. They can help you out of the deep rough, off bare lies, even out of fairway bunkers.

You don't need to hit your driver off every tee. Nor should you. Laura Davies, still probably the longest driver on the LPGA Tour, doesn't use her driver all that much. It is the most difficult club in the bag, and frankly a two- or a three-wood will fly higher and therefore a bit longer and will probably give you just as much distance as a driver. Because the driver is the longest club in the bag it's more unwieldy and easier to lose control of in the backswing, so don't pull your hair out if you can't get used to it—you have other power clubs in the bag that can get the job done equally well.

Likewise, the three-iron and the four-iron are both tough clubs to use. Again, you need more strength to use these clubs well than you need with a wood. A seven-wood will give you additional power and will get the ball out of the rough and in the air more quickly. When using an iron out of the rough, you need a steep angle of attack when you swing down on the ball and a firm grip to get the club face through the grass. But a wood that has a sole, and even rails on the bottom, has an easier time of it.

These days you don't have to choose between cut-down men's clubs and those itty-bitty toothpicks in the pink golf bag they call "ladies" clubs. Many women want to play with more athletic-looking equipment and they are demanding the best equipment.

In my opinion you should never settle for cut-down clubs, even if those clubs were the most expensive ones on the market. Simply put, cut-down men's clubs are too stiff and heavy, making it almost impossible for women to get much play out of them. It is harder to get the ball up in the air with a stiff shaft and you don't get the kick in the downswing that you want either. Because it takes more strength to swing the cut-down clubs, you get tired more quickly, too. Worst of all, you lose distance because it's impossible to generate enough clubhead speed with a cut-down club. All this, and I still haven't mentioned that the mere act of cutting a club down means you are changing all its measurements and it will no longer be balanced.

Just as when you buy a new pair of jeans or an expensive dress, you want your clubs to fit you. You want to make sure you feel comfortable with the flex in the shaft and the weight of the club—not too heavy, but not too light either. Most pros don't change their clubs very often. Like new shoes after they've been broken in, your clubs start to fit you the more you use them, and the more you use them the better they fit you. I had my last set of clubs for six years.

When you're choosing new clubs you also want to check the lie of the clubhead. My own clubs are fairly upright, about one or two degrees, but I'm pretty tall, and the more upright the club the stronger you have to be. If you hit all your shots off the heel of the club, that may be a sign

DON'T underestimate the importance of equipment. Educate yourself about what's best for you and your type of swing. Check for flex and weight—then go throw away that old pink golf bag!

that your clubs are too upright and you need ones with a flatter lie.

To test what kind of clubs you should buy, always try out the demos. That's what they're there for. You would never buy a pair of shoes without trying them on, or a car without driving it once, so don't even think about buying new clubs without swinging them first. Most stores will let you tape up the clubhead so that you can take some practice swings. This also gives you a chance to check the lie of the club. If the tape on the bottom of the club is rubbed off on the heel, then you know the club is too upright. If the tape is rubbed more toward the toe, then the clubs are too flat for you. Ideally, you want the tape on the bottom of the club to be rubbed smooth somewhere around the middle.

Now a lot of men probably would never admit this, but aesthetics play a big part in any new golf club purchase. For me, I have to like the face of the club. I like a rounded club face, a more open one. But you have to decide what you like best. It may sound silly, but if it looks uncomfortable, you're probably going to feel uncomfortable using it. If it looks smooth and sleek, the club is bound to boost your confidence. Admit it, you don't want to own a set of clubs so ugly that you feel as if you have to close your eyes every time you use them, do you?

Every Breath You Take

EXERCISING YOUR WAY TO BETTER GOLF

One of my biggest complaints about today's game is that too many people use golf carts when they could just as easily walk. I'm pretty sensitive to those comments about how golf isn't a real sport because you're never out of breath or you never break a sweat.

The value of physical fitness on the golf course is often underestimated. When you're physically fit, your focus, your concentration and your coordination are enhanced, and they are all significant elements in the game of golf. When you're fit, you also don't get as tired out on the golf course. And a tired golfer, we know, will often overswing.

I remember when I was part of the Swedish junior golf team that traveled to Wentworth, England, for the European Team Championships in 1981. We ran together for ten or fifteen minutes every day at about 7 A.M. In those days this was not such a common sight. The French and Italian teams were big smokers. They thought we were nuts. On Sunday, the last day of the competition, our coach made us go out and jog just to warm up and relax. I still believe that working up a good sweat before you go out to play is sometimes the best way to clear your mind, and God knows you need a clear mind to play good golf. For a lot of us on the Swedish team it obviously helped. We won the team championship.

A lot of people resist exercising, but if you play at least one other sport, I guarantee it will help your golf game. I started playing golf at age eleven, but I also was a big team handball player, rode horses, swam and played a lot of squash when I was growing up. I don't get to do very much of any of those extra sports anymore, but I do still run several times a week and work out on the exercise bike. All that exercise keeps me in shape, but it also keeps me in shape to play better golf. For women at risk for osteoporosis, there's also an obvious added health benefit to exercising your way to a better golf game.

Specific exercises can be especially helpful to women. Golf involves such monotonous, repetitive movements that when you work out it's important to even out your muscle groups by working the other side of your body—you know, all those muscles you don't use when you play golf.

For instance, if you're right-handed, taking practice swings left-handed should help your coordination. Here are some other specific exercises for specific parts of the body:

SHOULDERS: You can wear out your rotator cuff

pretty quickly in golf, the way pitchers often do in baseball. So it's important that you build strength in your shoulders. Lifting four- or five-pound free weights in each hand, by raising them up from your sides until they're on the same plane as your shoulders, will strengthen those shoulder muscles quickly. For the average female golfer, I suggest doing three reps of twelve each.

STOMACH: Posture is very critical to the golf swing, which is why strong stomach muscles are a must. (Strong stomach muscles will also relieve the pressure on your back, which is the area most often injured by golfers.) There are so many ridiculous ab-cruncher-type machines out there that are really superfluous—when all you need to do is the old-fashioned sit-up. Two sets of twenty-five each—or as many as you feel up to—are recommended. And you can always add more over time as you increase your stamina and strength.

LEGS: Since we discussed the importance of legs to the power swing earlier in the book, I should hope you all know by now that any exercise that works your thighs, in particular, is very important. I have a stationary bike at home, and when I travel I can usually find one either in a hotel gym or a local fitness center. (If you live in a cold weather climate, biking indoors is always a lot warmer, and a lot safer, too.)

ARMS/WRISTS: Having strong wrists and hands gives you a big advantage if you're trying to get more power out of

THIS is a great exercise for strengthening your arms, especially for women, since our upper bodies are not nearly as strong as our lower bodies. Hold your club by the grip and point it straight out at a right angle to, and parallel with, your left shoulder. Then write your name in the air with your club. Because you want your muscles to be balanced, repeat the exercise with your right arm.

your golf swing. Simply put, a strong grip requires strong hands and wrists. Doing curls with weights of three to five pounds is probably the best exercise. If you have a busy schedule and only have time to jog twenty minutes a day, then strap on a couple of those wrist weights while you run.

A Good Man Is Hard to Find

GOLF AND THE OPPOSITE SEX

At the Women's Open in Southern Pines, North Carolina, two years ago I had dinner with some guests of a corporate golf sponsor. One of them was remarking how she had played a round of golf earlier in the day with another woman who consistently hit her drives farther than she did. This upset the woman I was having dinner with because, as she explained, she was almost always longer off the tee than anyone else and so she couldn't figure out who this other woman was. A second dinner guest, who knew the mystery woman golfer in question, quickly explained that "she" was a "he" the year before!

Let's face it, men and women, even if they change their sexual identity, will always feel competitive with one another. When women tell me that it is sometimes frustrating to play golf with men, I tell them, "That's why we have handicaps." Handicaps will always level the playing field with a group of golfers of varying skills. But I know it doesn't do much to alleviate the intimidation factor. I always think the best way of breaking the ice is by using sarcasm, and saying something like "Aren't you lucky today, you get to play with a woman. Maybe you'll learn something."

Sometimes I've broken the ice inadvertently. I once played golf with the actor Sidney Poitier, who was very polite but somewhat reticent. I was sharing a cart (the club required them) with a female friend, and we decided to remove the windshield so that we could get some sun. With no place to put the windshield, we simply laid it at our feet. At some point in the round, while we were all mulling over our shots in the fairway, the cart suddenly took off on its own. The windshield had fallen against the gas pedal and the cart went careening down a hill out of control, with me in fast—but not fast enough—pursuit. Luckily the cart crashed into some bushes. It was a good thing, because I was laughing so hysterically I would have never caught up with it. I'm not sure what Sidney Poitier thought of me that day, but I know he had at least one good laugh.

It's amazing, though, how often *men* are the ones running away when they see a woman approaching their threesome on the first tee. The assumption is always that the woman golfer will slow them down. I know very fine women amateurs who still hear comments from men like "You play pretty good for a girl." Even when that "girl" is in her forties and has a 16-handicap.

The most important thing to remember is to play your own game. As women we have to get over the inhibition factor. More than likely, the men we play with are just as self-conscious as we are. They are usually so often caught up in the macho thing and not wanting to embarrass themselves that they're not even paying attention to how you're playing. Then again, sometimes they just embarrass themselves.

A few years ago I was playing in a pro-am in Japan where I was paired with the president of the Nichirei Corporation, which was sponsoring the LPGA tournament I was to play in that week. After stepping up to the first tee, he took a few practice swings, paused over the ball, then brought his club back and took a mighty . . . whiff. He actually fell on his butt! To his credit, he was a good sport about it—he kind of had to be—and laughed heartily. So did I.

It can be difficult, though, when you're paired with men who get really uptight when you're outplaying them. What I like to do, again, is be sarcastic in order to loosen things up. If I miss a putt, I might say, "Oops, my skirt blew up." If we can use our own sterotypes to joke about ourselves, we can make playing with men so much more comfortable. When we make fun of ourselves in this way we're also telling those guys who still say things like "Nice putt, Alice" when they miss a short one, that we know how they think. Women never talk disparagingly of men when *they* miss a putt. So when I'm playing with a male amateur, I'll kid with him

THE most important thing in golf—and in life—is to always have fun. If you can't laugh at yourself, well, then playing golf won't give you nearly the joy it should, and can. So when your putts aren't dropping and you're in the woods on every shot, remember: Lighten up!

when he misses a putt and say something like "Oh, did you drop your lipstick on that one?" Hopefully it sounds so ridiculous to him that we can both laugh at the joke. The bottom line is, playing golf isn't any fun if you're not having any fun playing.

It's Still Rock and Roll to Me

FINAL THOUGHT

Many people have written about how golf is like life, suggesting that if we only apply the lessons of life to golf, we'll learn to accept the game's peaks and valleys more readily. For me, though, it's the other way around. Golf is always teaching me about life, that my life is a wave and that I just have to go with it as best I can in order to survive it. Golf can be a constant battle to defeat fear, and in some ways life is, too.

But every time I'm down I learn something new and every time I'm up I value it more for what I've learned down below. Golf is about building something. The more shots you have, the more experience you have, the better your foundation and the higher you can go. Life is about building something, too. The more I know the better equipped I feel for whatever lies ahead.

Ultimately, of course, we may not be able to understand all of the twists and turns golf throws our way, nor all the sudden and often inexplicable obstacles of life. How do I explain, for instance, that the same clubs that I used to shoot a 63 in the U.S. Open one day, I used to shoot a 76 the next? I've come to the conclusion that in the final analysis golf is a game no one can completely understand. Which is maybe as it should be. Life, after all, is a mystery and what it gives us, the good and the bad, may in the end have more to do with destiny than self-determination.

If that sounds awfully fatalistic to some people, let me tell you it isn't, because I still believe that we are each responsible, as individuals, for putting ourselves in the hands of fate. How much control we do have over our own destinies may be beyond our ken, but that we *do* have control—over what and how much we put into life, into golf, and into the search for what we are each meant to do with it all—is assured.

In the same way, I've also come to realize that in order to get anywhere in golf or in life we have to be willing to give something extra. I was brought up to believe that nothing comes easy, that there is no free lunch. When I'm disappointed in myself or in my game, I've always pulled myself up and gotten my fighting spirit back.

Not winning the U.S. Open in 1994 wasn't the end of the world for me. If I win it someday, it probably won't be my greatest success either. I count my friends and the good times I've had with them and the competitive spirit that has never deserted me in golf or in all the other challenges I've faced in life, as my greatest gifts.

The rest is . . . rock and roll.